Y0-CAV-932

# Locked Up
# What To Do When
# Your AZZ Get's
# Locked Up

# A Poor Man's Guide
# To Freedom

## By

## Nancy Lockhart, M.J.

Copyright © 2011 Nancy Lockhart

All rights reserved.

ISBN: 146647677X
ISBN-13: 978-1466476776

# ACKNOWLEDGMENTS

I would like to thank my parents for instilling the creative abilities to think, analyze, reason, and live "outside the box".

Many thanks to my grandmother for teaching us the skills of survival at an early age.

Thank you Ms. Blue and The Blog Talk Remix Family for the birth of new energies, magical reinforcement and powerful creations.

Much appreciation to my ancestors, supporters, revolutionaries and activists.

Ahmed Gutale, Esq., Edward M. Brown, Esq. and Standish Willis, Esq. - your brilliance and dedication outshines the deceptive bowels of an unjust judicial system.

Carol Johnson Downs – your Loyola Law School friendship is forever appreciated. The Windy City would be void without you.

# CONTENTS

Nancy Lockhart, M.J.

## DISCLOSURE

The contents of this guidebook are not to be construed as legal advice. Legal advice should be obtained from a competent, licensed attorney. Please remember, all attorneys are **NOT** competent.

I am an expert Legal Analyst with years of grassroots organizing in the trenches. I hold a Master of Jurisprudence from Loyola University Chicago School of Law. I am not an attorney and the contents of this guide should not be construed as legal advice. - Nancy Lockhart, M.J.

LOCKED UP is designed as a guide for The Poor Man's Freedom.

# 1 STOPPED BY POLICE

## WHAT TO DO IF YOU ARE STOPPED BY POLICE

### Be Polite And Respectful At All Times

### KNOW YOUR RIGHTS

You have constitutional rights whether or not you're an American citizen.

You have the right to an attorney if you're arrested. Request one immediately.

You Have The Right To Remain Silent. Say so out loud so that the officer(s) hear you.

You have the right to refuse consent to search your person, your car and your home.

KEEP YOUR MOUTH SHUT – Be polite to police and do as you are told.

**Be Polite And Respectful At All Times!!!**

The police have a right to ask your name, date of birth and address. There could be exceptions to this rule. Give your name date of birth and show identification if requested ti show such. After that - KEEP YOUR MOUTH SHUT After That.

After you give your name, date of birth and address the police might read your miranda rights or mirandize you. When you have been mirandized, request an attorney. KEEP YOUR MOUTH SHUT. You have a right to remain silent. The Fifth Amendment of the United States Constitution gives you that right. You will not gain any grounds by trying to bargain with police. KEEP YOUR MOUTH SHUT. The police are not on your side.

ASK FOR AN ATTORNEY

It Can't BE Said Enough:

BE QUIET

SHUT UP

# DO NOT TALK

# REMAIN SILENT

# BE RESPECTFUL

# SHUT THE HELL UP

# ASK FOR AN ATTORNEY

If you talk, you could and probably will end up hurting yourself. In other words – ya might catch a bad case.

## What are Miranda Rights?

"You have the right to remain silent.

1. Anything you say can and will be used against you in a court of law.

2. You have the right to an attorney.

3. If you cannot afford an attorney, one will be appointed for you.

4. **Repeat:** If you cannot afford an attorney, one will be appointed for you."(www.findlaw.com)

## DO NOT RUN – DO NOT RESIST ARREST

Police are very suspicious that people who run have a weapon and if you run they may draw their weapon or, even shoot you in the back.

There are new cases everyday of police shooting individuals. Also, you will not be able to outrun the 30 plus officers and the helicopter that will chase you. If you run, your AZZ will more than likely be beaten when they catch you. Cops Are Wildin' Out. It's happening every day across the nation. If you are Black or, of Hispanic decent, your chances are greater.

Resisting arrest  - don't hit the officer, push the officer or, slap his hands away. What probably would have been a misdemeanor is now a felony because you touched the officer. You're headed to the penitentiary now for assault on an officer.

There is a great increase in unjustified police shootings and killings. Don't give the officer a reason to shoot you.

Keep your hands out of your pockets! You do not want to give the police the idea that there is a weapon in your pockets.

Keep your hands visible.

Remember the officer's name and badge number.

## WHAT TO DO **IF YOU ARE ARRESTED** AND TAKEN TO JAIL

You Have Rights and those rights include the right to remain silent. You will probably be questioned by police or, even interrogated. The cops may also beat you up. Request an attorney. This attorney should consult with you. Contact your loved ones or, friends and explain that you need an attorney.

Ask that your family assist in securing an attorney for you.

Depending on the severity of your charges, you may have your loved ones hire an experienced consultant to work with the attorney.

Explain your case to the attorney.

Remain polite to your attorney.

It seems perfectly legal for police to lie. It seems perfectly legal for the cops to beat arrestees for confessions. **Do not** let the cops trick you into signing a confession that you did not commit!

If there are others who were arrested with you, the police will more than likely come in and tell you that your friends have ratted you out or, snitched. Do not fall for this ancient tactic. Do so and you may be wrongfully convicted. Discuss your case with your attorney and only speak with the police through your attorney. This means that the lawyer should be sitting right beside you when you talk to the police.

If you cannot afford an attorney the state will appoint one for you. Many states have public defender's for the indigent.

Indigent means poor. Some states have both court appointed attorneys and public defenders. This varies from state to state. Whatever the case may be, if you cannot afford an attorney the state will provide one for you.

My experience has been that public defenders are very much overworked across the nation. Many are not able to provide proper representation for their clients because of case overloads.

### What Your Family and Loved Ones Need To Do

Your designated spokesperson should inform other family members and friends of the situation at hand. Your designated family member will need limited Legal Power Of Attorney to conduct business for you.

Give your loved one limited Power Of Attorney (POA)

Sit down and talk with an attorney.

Retain an attorney for your loved one.

Just because you have spoken with an attorney regarding your loved one, does not mean that he is going to represent your loved one. Get it in writing.

Talk with the attorney about a bond. There are four types of bonds and this varies from state to state. Find out from the attorney what the bond process should be.

As harsh as it may seem, your loved one may need to sit in the jail until trial. This is especially true if they don't have a job. Sitting in jail could free funds to pay a lawyer.

## Types of Bonds:

Personal Recognizance Bond

Cash Bond

Ten-percent Bond

Surety Bond

Determine from the attorney what type of bond may be needed. This will vary from state to state.

The attorney may be the only individual allowed to visit the jail initially. Determine what type communication you will have from the attorney. I've heard of cases where the public defender was so busy that (s)he was not able to visit the client until 10 months after the initial arrest. He sat in jail almost a year.

## Stop CALLING PEOPLE WHO CAN'T HELP GET YOUR AZZ OUTTA JAIL

Calling home wastes money whether it's via a phone card or, collect calls. The folks you're calling need to get a lawyer. Don't waste time and money talking to folk who can't get your azz outta the jail house. You can talk to these folks when you get out. If you don't get out and you sail up the river – you won't hear from these folks anyway. They will change their numbers and forget that you even exist.

Don't call your girlfriend, your baby momma, your play play mother in law and everybody else 10 times a day. Make your call to that person who is your spokesperson. Have them explain to the others that you need financial support for your legal defense.

# Stop Thinking **Everybody** Wants To Help **Your** AZZ

If you have a loving caring wife or husband, you might skip the next part.

Everybody does not want to help you. Stop thinking that everybody who says they will do anything in the world to help you means what they say.

Don't Nobody Wanna Save Your AZZ.

Call the loved one that you know will assist you and ask that individual to be the designated spokesperson for you.

Everybody Does Not Want To Help Save Your AZZ Remember that!

If your AZZ is gone up the river on lockdown for the next 10 years, your baby won't know you and your baby momma/daddy will have other baby momma's/daddy's by the time you get out.
**Remember That**

Two **Wrongs** Don't Make A Right

Don't sit there saying you want to get out of jail and you are in jail committing crimes. Do you actually want to get out or, are you just talking?

Don't waste your money, your loved one's money or anybody else's money sitting up in the jail house talking on an illegal cell phone, using drugs or anything else they told you not to do. Two Wrongs Don't Make A Right.

## GET YOUR MIND RIGHT

If you are reading this & you are incarcerated, get your mind right.

**That's important** – GET YOUR **MIND** RIGHT

Call On God, Jesus, Buddha, Allah, your Ancestors or whomever you normally call on. Ancestors are Uncle Tony who died last year, grandmother who passed long time ago and anyone else in your blood line who made the transition (died).

Other ancestors are those who worked in the trenches.

Get your mind right. Learn to play the game quickly.

## YOU **ONLY** GET ONE TIME TO MAKE A GOOD **IMPRESSION**

So, it's time for trial and you're overly anxious awaiting this date. Several very small things will make this stressful situation a lot smoother and more successful. Freedom For The Poor requires some work on your part.

Appearance – For Men - A short haircut will gain yourself positive results. If you have locks, a long wildin afro or braids. I suggest that you cut your hair into a very neat low (to the scalp) hair cut.

Now, I love locks, braids and semi wildin fros but, the judge and jury may not.

Have someone buy you a pair of pants that are your size – with a belt. If you have retained an attorney he would probably make this purchase for you and of course – add it to your bill.

If you have the public defender or, a court appointed attorney – chances may be slim. In that case – have your loved one go to a used clothing store and purchase a suit.. Most public defenders and court appointed attorneys have very limited budgets and low salaries.

During the trial, sit up straight in the chair, don't slouch down in the chair. Sit up straight and remain calm and cool – even if the police officer who arrested you lies.

## Appearance – For Women

Wear a skirt that is long enough to reach your knees. Wear a blouse that covers cleavage and your arms. I would remove long fake nails and the tall hair.

Don't walk in the court room with your orange thong showing cause your blue jeans are cut low and your orange shirt way above your belly.

Remember that you're seeking freedom – this is not a beauty contest or a swagin contest. This is a fight for your freedom.

Attitude – change your negative attitude. Call on your maker, your God or ancestors. Do whatever it is you have to do – change the negative attitude. Be respectful.

Never Give Up – Help yourself. Read, and take notes. Keep a journal with the facts of your case. Write notes in the Note Section of this book.

## 2 FAMILY FINANCES

### They Probably Are Not Rich

### Coupons Will Save Tremendously

Your designated spokesperson and other loved ones will experience financial hardship while assisting you. There are ways to save. You can certainly save with collect calls. Research companies that provide virtual local numbers. Your family members can make enormous savings using coupons. Learn the proper ways to use them.

## How To BEGIN Collecting Coupons

Sunday News Papers – no coupons on holidays.

On Line – Check The Internet

Swap With Friends and Family

Organize your coupons. Baseball card holders in a three ring binder works for me.  You may determine that filing inserts in folders, according to the date, works for you.

Locate stores that double coupons. Use your flyer for BOGO or buy one get one sales.

Use two coupons for BOGO if the store Policy allows.

This method of saving will give you additional money for gas and the many expenses that will arise as a result of your *LOCKED UP* loved one.

Do not let couponing force you into purchasing items that you honestly do not need and will not use. Use coupons to bring a savings to your current lifestyle while assisting your *LOCKED UP* loved one.

# Coupon Terms

## Learn The Terms

B1G1, BOGO, B1G1F = Buy One Get One Free

.25/1 == Twenty Five Cents off of One Item

IP = Internet Printable Coupon

MFR or MQ = Manufacturer's Coupon

PG, P&G = Proctor and Gamble Coupons (Sunday Inserts)

RP = Red Plum Coupons (Sunday Inserts)

SS = Smart Source (Sunday Insert)

Nancy Lockhart, M.J.

MIR = Mail In Rebate

WYB = When You Buy

NED = No Expiration Date

## Go To The Internet and Locate Stores In Your Area

Locate the store coupon policy – learn each store's policy, print the policy and place in your 3 ring binder. Carry it with you to the store.

## Keep Track Of Your Savings

Learn to stack coupons. Stacking is the use of more than one coupon per item. READ YOUR STORE'S POLICY! Each Store Policy is different. Some stores allow using one manufacturer's coupon, one store coupon and one competitor's coupon for one item.

## Example Of Stacking Coupons

Cereal XYZ is on sale for $2.45. That's a great savings from the normal $5.89. There is a store coupon in the store sale paper for $1.00 and you also have a manufacturer's coupon for $1.00 a competitor's coupon is not available.

The cost of XYZ cereal = .45

## 3 UNETHICAL LAWYER

### The Lawyer Sold Your AZZ Up The River

**What To Do When Your Lawyer Has Acted Unethically.** Your momma hired and paid a lawyer but your AZZ got 100 years in the joint and you're still maintaining your innocence. If you knew the lawyer had your case for one solid year and reviewed it the day before your trial – are you thinking (s)he did a good job?

If you have not heard from the lawyer the entire year you have a right to complain. Try to follow the chain of command, follow the structure.

Try to talk with the lawyer yourself. If that fails - request that your loved one's talk with this lawyer. If they are not satisfied you have a right to hire another one. You also have a right to file a complaint. You must prove that this lawyer did not work on your case or, that (s)he did not work to your benifit.

You're Stuck With The Lawyer AND..........Results were not great, you know (s)he did not put 100% into your case. Yep, (s)he did do a good job of sailing your AZZ up the river on a plea deal that was reduced from LIFE in prison to 100 years. Doesn't exactly sound like a deal does it?

What's the difference you ask? Life – either way you look at it – 100 years is Life in my opinion.

You have a right to file a complaint or grievance against this attorney. Each state has established a process. Locate your state's process and follow it. You must also gather up any evidence to support your complaint.

If you've paid this attorney to handle your case and your contract also includes hiring his private investigator but, (s)he did not – add that in your complaint and attach evidence of such.

Gather up everything that supports your claim and send it through tyour particular state's process.

You might also try contacting the judge's law clerk. A law clerk is a lawyer who assists the judge by conducting important research. A judge's law clerk is not a secretary.

It appears to be very hard in some states to sue an attorney but, it's not impossible. You may need to retain an attorney to sue the attorney who sent your AZZ up the river for 100 years. Find coupons for hotels, gas, food, clothes, personal items, rental cars, airline tickets, train tickets and restaurants.

Meanwhile – you need to file an appeal, post conviction motion or, whatever else you haven't filed and you need the services of an attorney.

Ask your family to interview an attorney. Observe how respectful (s)he is.

If the lawyer has an attitude problem and is disrespectful so to speak, (s)he may not be the attorney for you.

If (s)he's stern but confident – this may be the right one. Ask about (s)his track record. Research the attorney on the internet. Inquire about other cases handled. Ask questions. If you find that many of his clients are in **prison** – I'd reconsider. If he's only handled civil cases – be careful – would you want an eye doctor performing surgery on your gall bladder? UMMM! What about a dentist delivering your first child? Not saying here that both are impossible but, medical doctors specialize and attorneys specialize.

Find one that is passionate about what (s)he does. Ask them how they are going to assist your loved one. Determine their strategies and ask about an appeal. Remember that the highest court in the US is the Supreme Court. **If an attorney tells you that there are no additional remedies after the court of appeals – find out why (s)he's saying that.**

## Ineffective Assistance of Counsel

You will normally have a right to raise the claim of ineffective assistance of counsel before your trial begins. This claim has to be a truthfully substantial claim – such as ineffectively being prepared, no field investigations, etc. - the trial court has a constitutional duty to investigate your claim. Pre-trial ineffective assistance claims are treated much more differently than post-trial claims. **So, if you say something before the trial it is much better treated than, if you say something later – on appeal.**

If you do not raise a claim before your trial you may certainly do so immediately after and before sentencing.

In some cases a hearing will be conducted. This depends on your state rules. However done, make sure that it's done. Attorneys should not act unethically. The judge will ask you about your representation at the end of the trial. Telling the truth then can possibly save you some troubles during the appeals process.

If information is not included in the lower court trial – it normally cannot be brought up on appeal.

The Innocence Project - (http://www.innocenceproject.org/understand/Bad-Lawyering.php) discusses causes of DNA Overturned Cases. The following is presented to you as a direct quote from (http://www/innocenceproject.org).

The resources of the justice system are often stacked against poor defendants.

Matters only become worse when a person is represented by an ineffective, incompetent or overburdened defense lawyer.

The failure of overworked lawyers to investigate, call witnesses or prepare for trial has led to the conviction of innocent people.

When a defense lawyer doesn't do his or her job, the defendant suffers. Shrinking funding and access to resources for public defenders and court-appointed attorneys is only making the problem worse.

**Asleep on the job**
A review of convictions overturned by DNA testing reveals a trail of sleeping, drunk, incompetent and overburdened defense attorneys, at the trial level and on appeal.

And this is only the tip of the iceberg.

Innocent defendants are convicted or plead guilty in this country with less than adequate defense representation. In the some of the worst cases, lawyers have:

- slept in the courtroom during trial
- been disbarred shortly after finishing a death penalty case

- failed to investigate alibis
- failed to call or consult experts on forensic issues
- failed to show up for hearings

Good Defense Means Fair Justice

There are ways to stop wrongful convictions from occurring as a result of ineffective representation.

See our Fix The System section to learn more about our recommendations in support of better defense for poor defendants."

**Personal NOTE:** If you were convicted of a crime and your attorney states that you have exhausted all of your appeals - you may want to consider a post-conviction motion that petitions the state court or the federal court for a Writ of Habeas Corpus. Basically, a Writ of Habeas Corpus will attack the conviction or sentence on constitutional grounds.

More simply stated, you will argue that the conviction or, the sentence violates the constitution and should be over turned.

**ALSO REMEMBER:** Each state has a Supreme Court and The United States Supreme Court is the highest court of the land.

## 4 BABY MAMMA BABY DADDY DRAMA

### How To Keep Your AZZ Out The Pitfalls Of Child Support

## There Is No Need To Sit There Chillin And You Do Not Have A Job

### You Are Still Required To Pay For The Child!

### If You Don't Pay – YOUR AZZ WILL BE LOCKED UP!

You've just realized that your ex-wife, baby momma or, baby daddy ........ is living with another person.

You refuse to make child support payments because in your head you see "your money" supporting another man/woman. You refuse to make the child support payment(s). Bad Move!

On the other hand – John down the street is stressing it because his ex lost her job and he thinks she's using the child support to get her hair and nails done with "his money". John decided to stop paying. Guess what? It's not John's decision.

You can't do that. If you Don't Pay – Your AZZ Will Be Locked UP!

The Non Custodial Parent means the parent who does **NOT** have custody of the child. In other words, the parent who is not keeping the child. A non custodial parent can go to jail for not paying child support. Even if you lost your job, you can go to jail for not paying child support. Even if you're waiting for disability to "kick in" – you can go to jail for not paying child support. When you come out of the joint – you will still owe child support.

**And the kid don't know you from Joe Blo!**

No, it's got nothing to do with what your ex, or baby mama told the kid. Not one Damn thing!

Your AZZ was absent during the kid's life and they simply will NOT KNOW YOUR AZZ!!

The kid will just **NOT KNOW YOUR AZZ!**

**Children Suffer The Most!!**

## The Child Support Order

The child support order is a legally binding document from the court. It is normally signed by the judge. The child support order tells: when you pay – how much you pay and how often you pay child support to the custodial parent. That parent is normally your ex wife, baby momma, the baby grand momma, baby daddy or, the state. You may have to pay the state because the child is in foster care or, something of that nature.

Normally, you are required to pay child support until the child (children) turn(s) 18 years of age. You may have to pay after the child turns 18 if you're behind on payments. In other words – if you have been in prison for 16 years – your child support went like this – CHA CHING, CHA CHING$$$.

How Can I Change The Child Support Order? The courts can change it but You cannot.

So, you've lost your job and cannot afford to pay the amount as ordered. Unemployment isn't enough – if you're fortunate enough to receive it or, you may not have an income at all! No matter the situation- Don't just Chill – Your AZZ Will Get Locked Up!!

Modifying The Child Support Order – My comparative analysis yields the easiest way to make changes(modify),  the order is for both parents to agree. If you both agree request that the judge modify the order.

## What To Do When Your AZZ Getz Locked Up

Locate the appropriate office in your respective state and county. **In other words – look in the phone book and find the right office.**

Look under your county's family court website or, look under the Department of Social Services website. Locate a phone number and forms. The form may be titled "Petition To Modify Child Support Form" Fill the forms out. Don't give them to your new girl/guy to hold for you. Don't trust her/him to fill them out and mail them. See about this yourself. Do this yourself - cause If you just Chill – Your AZZ Will Get Locked up!! **The new girl/guy will forget about you when they ship you up the river!**

Don't be afraid to ask for help!

Don't Push Up On The Clerk and Catch Another Case!

Ask the clerk to assist you with locating the proper form(s).

You will probably also need a financial statement form.  Remember – this is not legal advice – this information is solely my opinion. You may need to seek the services of an attorney.

Another way of making changes (modifying) the court order is by asking the court to modify the order. This is normally done by a court hearing. You probably need to seek the services of an attorney at this point.

It's best to try and stomach your ex so that you both come to an agreement.  It's easiest on your pockets in the long run and doesn't hurt the child as much. Children suffer when parents argue and fight.

Remember – If you hit your ex – you will probably have Your AZZ Locked Up! -- Now you have even more legal problems. More MONEY!

You're headed up the river. You Caught Another Case!

**See Chapter I – What To Do When Your AZZ GET'S LOCKED UP!** Don't get indignant, start wildin out, or, act a complete jack **AZZ** when you learn that you must pay a filing fee to modify your child support orders. Remain polite.

The clerk at the window didn't make these rules – (s)he's there to carry out the plan and didn't create the plan.

Don't go to jail for cussing out the child support clerk.

## Bankruptcy and Child Support

You're talking to one of your boys and he tells you to file bankruptcy to make the child support payment go away.

I don't get this - the kid ain't going away!

Anyhow – child support payments don't vanish with bankruptcy. Save your time, money and energy.

Child support payments are normally based on your income.

Don't Chill – Your AZZ is Going To Get Locked Up!!

**Everybody's Moving To Different States**

So, your ex has moved to another state and you're moving to a totally different. The child support order was in the state that the two of you hooked up in to have the kid – which state prevails? Well, there is an Act called the Uniform Interstate Family Support Act which governs this type of situation.

Start with the state that you hooked up with your ex, or, baby momma in. Go to the Internet and find the Act – read it!! Again, it's called the Uniform Interstate Family Support Act.

**Get all of your documents together and don't take a year to do that** –documents include financial statements, proof of paying for your child's health insurance, proof that you were laid off or, fired.

What To Do When Your AZZ Getz Locked Up

(Remember, the judge probably does not want to know a long story about what "They Said You Did" to get fired) **IF you Chill – Your AZZ is Going To Get Locked Up!**

So, what's next? What do you do? Don't Chill – Your AZZ is Going To Get Locked up! Try cutting some grass and raking some yards and get the child support paid before it's too late. Pay it until you have a new Order.  Do small odds and ends to keep it going.  Learn how to use coupons. There is a scientific strategy for using coupons.

Learn that strategy by listening to The Nancy Lockhart Show archives on

Blog Talk Radio. That URL (website address) is below.

http://www.blogtalkradio.com/thenancylockhartsho w/2011/10/13/toomuchdoubt-troy-davis-mumia-abu-jamal-family-finances

Listen to October 13, 15,  20, and 27th of 2011 archives.

Nancy Lockhart, M.J.

Couldn't get the child support order modified?
Speak with an attorney about appealing the
decision. Use a combination of hard work and
coupons to get through this.

## 5 YOUR AZZ CAN'T DRIVE

**What To Do To Avoid The Pitfalls of Catching Another Moving Violation Case. Don't Go Into Denial! Your License was snatched and your AZZ is still drivin.**

You acted a fool, drove drunk and lost your State issued driver's license. So, you don't have a driver's license and you're considering using a bicycle or a moped. No matter your choice, learn the state and county (NOT COUNTRY) law for operating a bicycle or a moped in your place of residence. Do not drive without license and insurance.

Nancy Lockhart, M.J.

You're asking for more trouble and possibly lots of time in the joint.

Some States require that you use a bicycle helmet while riding. Some states also require that you ride on the street. Most states DO NOT allow riding a bicycle on major highways such as the interstate. Learn the requirements! You do not need to have a ticket on top of the many fines and SR22 insurance for reinstating your driver's license.

Some states do not allow riding a bicycle on business zone sidewalks but, many do allow riding on the sidewalks of residential neighborhoods.  Most states require the bicyclist learn the proper hand signals.

You may obtain alternate forms of identification in the form of a passport or state issued identification card.

If you've chosen to ride a moped – make sure that you've read your respective state's moped operating handbook. Follow the rules.

You must be examined for the moped operator's license so, study and know the laws. If you are not able to understand – ask for assistance from a friend or loved one.

Don't worry about them laughing at you.

It's best to be laughed at on THIS SIDE OF THE WALLS!

## TERMS

**DUI** – Driving Under The Influence

**DWI** – Driving While Intoxicated

**SSI** - Disability that you will probably need to apply for since you're permanently in a wheel chair from getting banged up while crashing into that angel oak tree after drinking shine at Pookie dem's house. You don't have an income and you need funds to survive. You may need to apply after you've served the time for killing an innocent person cause your AZZ was drunk behind the wheel.

**SR22 Insurance** – Expensive Insurance that you will probably need to drive again because of the DUI.

**DUI Second** – more time and money for driving drunk again.

**DUI Third** – even more time and money for driving drunk again for the 3$^{rd}$ time. You will probably spend a good bit of time in the joint.

**Vehicular Manslaughter** – is the charge you caught when you left Pookie dem's house after drinking that apple pie, running 'cross the highway and killing Bubba's wife and kids. Now your AZZ is in prison in a wheelchair.

# 6 GUNS, BULLETS & FELONS

## How To Avoid The Pitfalls Of Illegal Gun Ownership

### Concealed Weapons Permits

Individual States are not regulated by the Federal Government for carrying weapons. However the Federal Government does regulate Felons. Many states in the U.S. Have passed laws that allow individuals to carry a concealed weapon – either with a permit or without. It is your responsibility to know the laws in the state that you reside. Additionally, it is YOUR responsibility to know the laws of states that you are traveling through.

In other words, know the law for that weapon in your car or, on your person. Don't take Uncle Jimmy Ray's word – do the research. If your state requires a permit to carry a gun - follow procedures for obtaining such.

## GUNS AND CONVICTED FELONS

Anyone who has been convicted of a felony is banned by federal law from ever possessing "any firearm or ammunition." Specifically a person "convicted in any court of a crime punishable by imprisonment for a term exceeding one year" cannot possess any firearm in any location. 18 U.S.C. 922(g) is the federal law that prohibits anyone ever convicted of any felony to ever possess any firearm either inside or outside of his home. The federal punishment for felon gun possession is up to 10 years in prison.

There are many other federal gun ownership restrictions.

A good summary is available from the Bureau of Alcohol Tobacco, Firearms and Explosives.

# Your Personal Notes

.

Nancy Lockhart, M.J.

# Your Personal Notes

# ABOUT THE AUTHOR

Nancy Lockhart, M.J., is a non attorney legal analyst with a sincere passion for researching and publicizing wrongful convictions and issues of grave injustices.

Lockhart is most notably recognized for her work in freeing The Scott Sisters.
(http://www.nancylockhart.blogspot.com)
(http://www.nancylockhart.net)

She created and lead a movement along with Mrs. Evelyn Rasco – mother of The Scott Sisters. That movement became a viral, global movement via social networking and field organizing by utilizing creative planning with online and off line organizing strategies.

Nancy Lockhart, M.J.

Lockhart holds a Master of Jurisprudence from Loyola University Chicago School of Law where she supported herself by working as a consultant for Rainbow PUSH Coalition. At PUSH, Lockhart initially championed the cause of The Scott Sisters. Upon graduation from Loyola University Chicago School of Law, and leaving PUSH, Lockhart continued and successfully obtained freedom for The Scott Sisters with their mother – Mrs. Evelyn Rasco.

As a third generation public school teacher, Lockhart followed the tradition of creating "outside the box" teaching strategies for students with learning disabilities and emotional problems. Her consciousness and disapproval of the "school to prison pipeline " led her to work with juvenile delinquents.

As a Reader's Digest DeWitt Wallace Fellow – Lockhart refined strategies to integrate technology and writing.

 The _Locked Up_ series is a tool against mass incarceration.

# A Post Script

## FROM Corporate Governance

## TO

## ORGANIZING IN THE TRENCHES

Printed In Black Commentator.com (November 20, 2008 - Issue 300**)**

**The State of Mississippi versus Jamie Scott and Gladys Scott:**

**My First Encounter with Justice Denied**

**By Nancy R. Lockhart, M.J.**

BlackCommentator.com **Guest Commentator**

While driving the moving truck from South Carolina to Chicago, Illinois in July of 2005, many things ran across my mind as I took the solo trip. I pondered receiving the Master of Jurisprudence degree from Loyola University School of Law and later a career as a governmental regulatory compliance manager. It never dawned on me that I would receive a brutal education in social justice; an education that would prove to be more valuable than sheepskin from any institution.

This would become an education that re-directed every thought flowing as I drove that big truck from South Carolina.

I left Chicago with the Master of Jurisprudence and absolutely no desire to follow my original dreams.

I secured a position as a Community Services Consultant with Rainbow/PUSH Coalition while completing my studies. I will never forget the frigid, Chicago morning when I opened a letter from Mrs. Evelyn Rasco, a mother and widow. She told the story of her daughters, and said she had written Rainbow/PUSH for 11 years, without a response.

She redirected her strategy this time and wrote Congressman Jackson in a plea to get the letter to his father's (Rev. Jackson) office. The letter was hand delivered. I called Mrs. Rasco and promised to get back in touch. Her approach is consistently that of a persistent mother – determined to secure help for her two daughters, who are serving double life terms each, in the state of Mississippi, for armed robbery.

*Allegedly, 9, 10, or 11 dollars was stolen. No one was injured, murdered or taken to the hospital.* Though often discouraged, I've found out, through my interactions with Mrs. Rasco, that she is rich in perseverance and her belief in God.

The following months would comprise of in-depth research efforts, on my part, on behalf of the Scott sisters.

After reading the transcripts, as well as other documents, many times, I spoke with various legal experts – one of whom passed away before completely assisting with the case. Subsequently, I was convinced that a grave injustice had been wrought from the judicial bench. This injustice has proven to be the misrepresentation of poor Black women seeking justice in Mississippi's legal system.

Justice was denied. I left Chicago with a commitment to somehow free Jamie and Gladys Scott. The parents of Jamie and Gladys Scott had felt that life for the family would be better in Mississippi than in Chicago. They had left the Chicago South Side and moved to Mississippi. Instead of finding a more peaceful, safe environment, they found a racist town where the white man's spoken word is the law and justice for poor Black people, absent.

On December 24, 1993, Scott County Sheriff's Department arrested the sisters for armed robbery. *In October of 1994, Jamie and Gladys Scott were sentenced to double life terms in prison. That's double sentences each! Neither sister had prior convictions.* Three young Black men confessed to the robbery, but implicated Jamie and Gladys in the crime.

The three young men, all related and ranging from ages 14 to 18, confessed to committing the crime. Coercions, threats and promises later led these men to turn state's evidence on the Scott Sisters.

The 14-year-old testified that he signed a written statement without an attorney present.

He was told that he would be sent up to Parchman Farm – the notorious Mississippi Penitentiary/Plantation – if he did not cooperate. In addition, he was told that he would be "made out of a woman" (raped by

men) at Parchman. The 14-year-old witness had spent 10 months in jail and was, at this point, ready to get out. His confession was a condition of entering a plea agreement for strong-armed robbery, which does *not* carry a life sentence. The 14-year-old *never read* the statement. He only signed it.

In 1998, one of the Patrick Men wrote an affidavit telling the truth – that Jamie and Gladys were not involved. The court never heard the affidavit. There are presently three affidavits which state that Gladys and Jamie had nothing to do with this robbery.

According to the Request for Commutation of Sentence and/or Pardon prepared by attorney Chokwe Lumumba, the Scott Sisters challenged their convictions on direct appeal; arguing that there was insufficient evidence to convict them, and the guilty verdict was against the overwhelming weight of evidence, which should exonerate them.

The court of appeals found no error and affirmed the convictions on December 17, 1996. As a result, they filed a Petition for Writ of Certiorari to the Supreme Court, which was denied on May 15, 1997.

They consequently filed an Application for Leave to File Motion to Vacate Conviction pursuant to the Mississippi Post Conviction Collateral.

Relief Act. The Supreme Court also denied that application.

The attorneys from the lower court failed to interview and subpoena witnesses for the hearing. The jury never heard the testimony from the victims. Their attorney only called one witness, when there were several. The sisters did not testify on their own behalf, because both their attorneys advised them not to. The attorneys failed to interview and subpoena the witnesses. The affidavits of 3 witnesses were newly discovered evidence, and were unknown during the lower court trial. Attorney Chokwe Lumumba submitted a request for commutation of sentence and pardon to governor Musgrove. It was denied.

Gladys and Jamie's older brother served in Iraq for the US Army, while Americans wrongfully placed his sisters in prison on double life terms each.

No one was murdered, injured or taken to the hospital. Their mother and children have suffered extensively from justice denied.

## DISCLOSURE

The contents of this guidebook are not to be construed as legal advice. Legal advice should be obtained from a competent, licensed attorney. All attorneys are **NOT** competent. Do your homework.

13888414R00032

Made in the USA
Charleston, SC
07 August 2012